Lincoln's Medieval Jewry — and Up-hill — Norman Houses

SECOND EDITION

Written by

Maureen Birch

ISBN 978-1-907516-32-0

Published by: TUCANNbooks, 19 High Street, Heighington, Lincoln LN4 1RG
Tel & Fax: 01522 790009
www.tucann.co.uk

This book is dedicated to the late Stan Warmoth, Rev. John Wilford, my husband Neville and Joan Kendall

Contents

Jews Court/Jews House in late 19th Century from 'This England'

FOREWORD

Most ancient buildings have a story to tell and it is sometimes curiosity, growing into fascination and affection that tempts a local historian to delve deeper and deeper. This little booklet, by a long-standing member and officer of the Society for Lincolnshire History and Archaeology, is a labour of love. Maureen Birch does not claim to tell the whole story of Jews Court, nor the complete history of the Jews in Lincoln. She did not set out to write an academic treatise or a scholarly reference book. Her driving inspiration was simply her own curiosity whilst working in Jews Court and seeking to answer the wide range of questions posed by countless visitors.

What Maureen has produced is a colourful series of sketches, or pictures, that have caught her imagination. Each one features Jews Court and people over the ages for whom Jews Court was important. She takes us back in time to the first Jews who settled in our city, transformed the local economy, and built synagogues amongst the churches of medieval Lincoln. Her story is one of a hard-working prosperous community rewarded with persecution and banishment. But Jews Court survived as a monument, used and often abused, knocked down and rebuilt, but standing always as a witness and memorial to the Jewish community that built it and first worshipped in it. On behalf of the Chairman and Trustees of the Jews Court Trust I am honoured to commend this little booklet as a welcome contribution to the history of Lincoln.

Rev. John Wilford FSA

ACKNOWLEDGEMENTS

My sincere and grateful thanks go to all those who have helped in any way towards the production of this booklet. The late Stan Warmoth, Rev. John Wilford, Chris Johnson, and the staff of Lincolnshire County Archives Catriona Wheeler, Michael Jones, Joan Kendall, John Herrick, Bernard Sullivan, Mrs. Mould, (who kindly allowed me to interview her), the late David Vale (for his splendid picture), my husband Neville (for his help and guidance and editing), Karen Gennard, Don & Audrey Gould, Michael Needham, Susan Smith, the late Don Dowson and the many friends at Jews Court who have encouraged me.

Adrian James of *The Society Of Antiquaries Of London.*

Michael Sassi, Editor of *The Lincolnshire Echo.*

The Editor of *This England.*

Jim Garretts, Director of the *Manchester Jewish Museum.*

Shirley Goldzweig, the Montagu Centre Administrator of the *Peggy Lang Centre for Jewish Education*

City of Lincoln Archaeology Unit

The Jews Court Trust

The Staff of the *Local Studies Department, Lincoln Central Library*

To the Dean and Chapter of Lincoln

ILLUSTRATIONS

I am deeply indebted to all the above who have so willingly allowed me to use their illustrations and photographs.

INTRODUCTION

At the foot of Steep Hill many visitors stop to look at an impressive pair of stone buildings: Jews House and Jews Court. Often mistaken for one building these properties catch the imagination of the tourist and prompt many people to ask about their history. Arising from their names, and creating just as much interest, a second question follows:
"Please can you tell us about Lincolns Medieval Jewry?" This is an attempt to answer these questions, and is for all those visitors who have requested a booklet and, especially, to those who have encouraged its publication.

Note: Within each chapter references are made to numbers eg (2). These refer to a list of references which appear at the end of the book. They may be useful for further research.

CHAPTER 1
The Jews return to Jews Court

TWENTIETH CENTURY BETROTHAL

On Sunday 12th January 1992 a very special, and historic, event took place at Jews Court which was to link twentieth century Lincoln to the city's medieval past. During the twelfth and thirteenth centuries Lincoln was second only to London in having in its midst the largest number of Jews resident in England. One important recorded event is that of a betrothal in 1271 which took place between Judith, the daughter of Bellasez, and Aaron, the son of Benjamin of Lincoln. Traditionally Bellasez was said to have lived at Jews House and the Shiddukhim (betrothal) took place in the synagogue next to the house, and there exists a strong tradition that Jews Court stands on the original site of this synagogue.

A document, in Westminster Abbey Muniment Rooms, records this ceremony and describes how the wedding took place in 1275.

An extract from Adlers transcript of the betrothal contract says: *'The said Bellase; has betrothed her daughter Judith the daughter of Hayim [Hagin] to Aaron the son of Benjamin upon the following conditions... 'The said Bellasez promised to the said Aaron as a dowry twenty marks sterling and the 24 books [of the Bible] properly provided with punctuation and the Masora and written upon calf-skin.'* (1)

It was this ceremony, vividly described by historian Cecil Roth, that so impressed a young couple, Clive Wolman, city editor of *The Mail on Sunday*, and Anna Roden, a financial manager at Warburgs, that they decided to hold their betrothal at Jews Court. The date was set as near as possible to the date of the medieval ceremony, and was the first such ceremony since the Jews were expelled from England in 1290.

The participants were taken back in time as four Jewish lawyers read an official document relating to the 13th century betrothal. John Wilford, a member of the Jews Court Trust, described how each guest was offered a copy of the original betrothal contract along with an English transcript (2) Amongst the gifts exchanged were a copy of the Bible (Old Testament) and five cookery books from Anna's mother, the cookery writer Claudia Roden. (3)

This service inspired a group of members of the Nottingham Liberal and Progressive Synagogue to call a meeting at the Friends Meeting House in Lincoln. In 1993 a report in a county newspaper told how this meeting attracted 60 people, from which a committee was formed in order to institute a Jewish Community in Lincoln. (4) The group approached the Jews Court Trust and then the Executive Committee of the Society for Lincolnshire History and Archaeology with a request that they be allowed to hold their fortnightly meetings at Jews Court. So it was that in September 1992 a Jewish Community assembled in Lincoln, to hold the first meeting since the Jews were expelled from England in 1290; they have met regularly ever since. In 1996 the Jews obtained permission to place a small commemorative plaque in the room where they meet. This reads:

This Plaque Commemorates the Return of the Jewish Community
To Lincoln on 12th September 1992 (14 Elul. 5752)

This return surely brings back thoughts of when the early Jews first came to Lincoln.

CHAPTER TWO
Medieval Jewry 1066-1290

And where that the Jews were in auncieaunt tyme enhabettaunt [inhabited] in the seyd rede [road] all theyre merchaundyse [merchandise] to be solde as Lumbdn[lumber?] doth at this daie [day] in your Cite of Londn, and as it nowe [now] schewith [showeth] that the grettest [greatest] heidplacez [highplaces] were of theyre beildyngez [buildings], as in a boke [book] of your Exchequer of record itt appereth [appeareth]; and now the grenowmbre [?] of the seyd [said] heidplacez be wasted an desolate fr [for] lakke [lack] of inhabytautez [inhabitants] and be... void groundez... (1)

So reads part of a petition, that the citizens of Lincoln presented to Richard III (1483/5), which showed something of the impact of medieval Jews upon the city. The Jews had come to London from Rouen with William the Conqueror in 1066. The first known reference to Lincoln's Jews appears in 1159: 'when the sheriff accounted for £40 for them. ' (2) It looks as if Lincoln did not 'lakke [the J inhabytaute:' of the Jewish Community: for the Jews House, Jews Court and the Norman House stand as proof of their presence.

The question arises: where did these Jews live? Joseph Jacobs writing about the London Jewry said: almost all the English Jewries were situated near the chief market and mentions that 'in Lincoln the synagogue adjoined the market'. His evidence came from Lincoln Cathedral charters and monastic cartularies, which confirm that 'several Jews were gathered near the high market in St Michaels parish ': including Ursell the Jew who had property just outside the Bail's south gate, with Moses, son of Benedict, holding land nearby. (3) As may be seen from the map (Fig. 3) Lincoln had several markets: i.e. skin, poultry, fish, corn and drapery, each in its own location. Tradition also holds that there was a Bullring. (4) Lincoln Jews held properties in other areas of the city such as the Wigford suburb. Ursell Levy, owned houses in the parish of St. Marks, and another, Jacob Levi, in St. Benedicts. (5)

Lincoln's Medieval Jewry and up-hill Norman houses

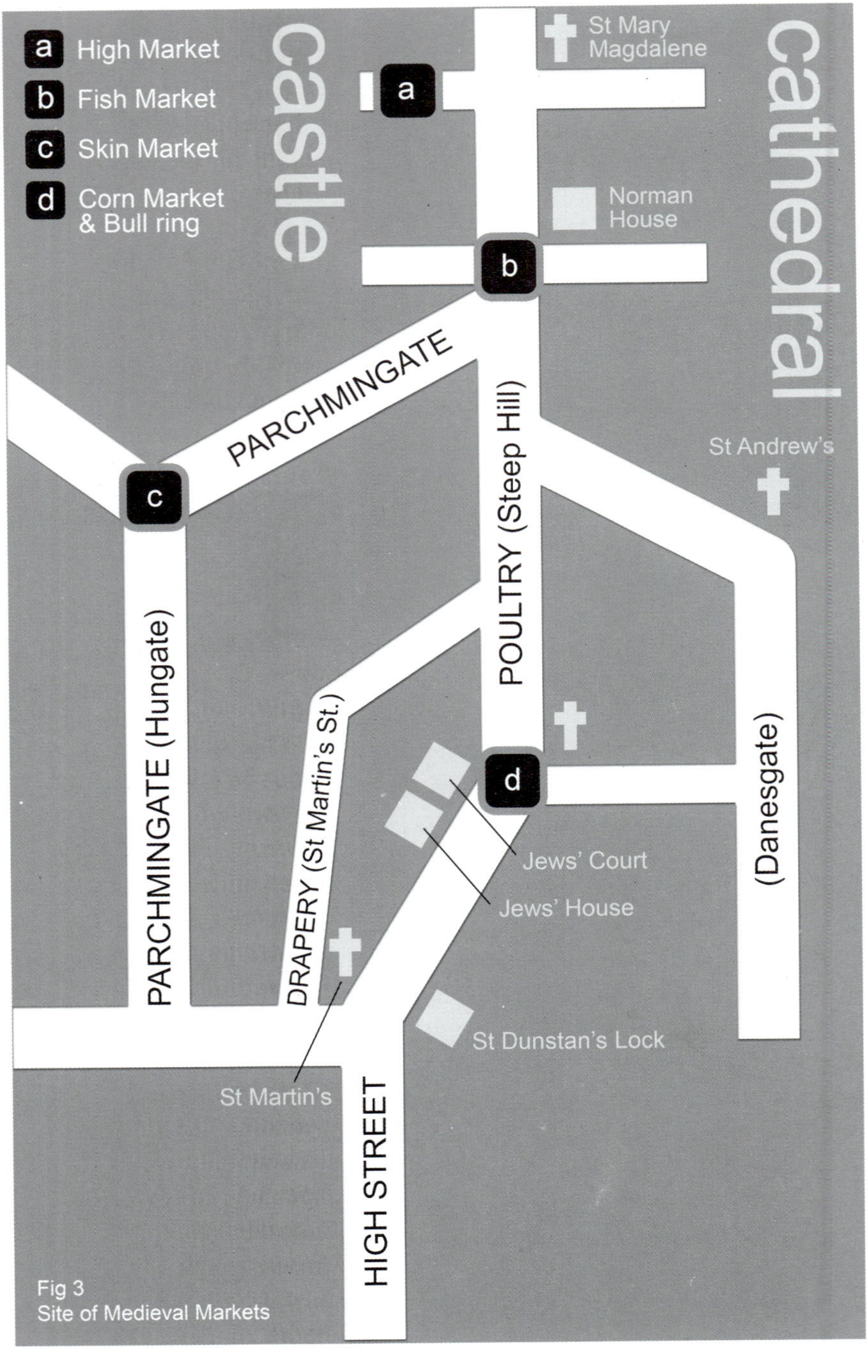

Fig 3
Site of Medieval Markets

A popular belief is that there was a Jewish ghetto (segregated area) in Lincoln, but there is no conclusive evidence. How did this arise? One theory put forward, by Sir Charles Anderson, was his reference to a barrier which was 'placed across the entrance of the Strait and secured at night'. (6) Another local historian, E.I. Abell, in a letter to the local press, said that 'there was no evidence of a ghetto in Lincoln', and described the nightly closing of Dernestall Lock [at the entrance to The Strait] as 'a myth'. (7) Sir Francis Hill in pursuing this question argued that as the Strait is part of the main highway joining the upper city to the lower it would be ridiculous to suppose that it could be barred at night. He further points to documentation that makes it plain that Jews lived on either side of this imaginary barrier. Another local historian, MD Davis, favoured the Bail as the site of a ghetto, as that would be under the protection of the constable of the castle. (8) However, protection does not necessarily prove a ghetto, and no documentation exists to back up the theory of a ghetto in Lincoln.

Although names and addresses of Jews residing in Lincoln may be found in such records as The Calendar of Patent Rolls little is known about many of them. The most well - known by far is Aaron of Lincoln, (sometimes known as Aaron of York), who was immortalised by Sir Walter Scott in his novel 'Ivanhoe'. Aaron, an astute money -lender, made his name as the most enterprising Jew in England between 1166 and 1185. Because medieval Christians were not allowed to lend money for profit, and as most occupations and organisations were closed to the Jews, money lending was one of the few lucrative options left open to them. Jews were unable to join craft guilds as their faith prevented them from taking the required Christian oaths. Aaron's popularity grew as he became valued for his business expertise as much as for his financial aid. Abbeys, priories and churches were indebted to him as he realised a great potential in the marketing of wool. He also assisted many members of the nobility, even the King.

Aaron was indeed a valuable asset to Lincoln, where the Cathedral authorities had good reason to be grateful to him for his financial aid in the rebuilding, by Bishop Hugh, of the Cathedral after the earthquake of 1185. There is no doubt that Aaron was very wealthy but the money he loaned and invested need not have all come out of his own pocket. He was possibly a sort of medieval investment broker using money belonging to other people as well as his own.

Lincoln's Medieval Jewry and up-hill Norman houses

There is no doubt that many people borrowed money from Aaron. Sir Francis Hill tells how in 1165/6 Henry II owed Aaron £29-8s-10d; *and after Aarons death nine Cistercian Abbeys were found to be in debt to him*. An account tells of a miller of Washingborough, William son of Fulk, founder of a chantry in Lincoln Cathedral, who owed £68-1s-4d secured on his mill. A promissory note in the Public Record Office records how, in 1179, the parson at Bisebrok (Rutland) owed Aaron *25 soams of hay, Stamford Measure*. The note promised that the parson had agreed that *every two loads shall make one great bundle, Lincoln measure, and all this corn I will render him within fifteen days of his summons*. This note showed how Aaron sometimes dealt in hay, another marketable commodity. When Aaron died a very rich man in 1186, it was Henry II who seized his property. Ironically while his valuables were being transported to Normandy the ship sank in mid-channel.(9)

In 1997 Ivanhoe was televised. Upon its showing, the late Dr. Dorothy Owen and Professor John Gillingham (London School of Economics), criticised some of the inadequacies of the production. Dr. Owen pointed out that, although the Jews were very cut off socially, they were in other respects, very much integrated into the community. This fact was quite rightly emphasised in the novel itself. She also emphasised how the role of Jews as money-lenders played an essential part in the economic life of Lincoln. (10)

There is no doubt that the Jews influenced the prosperity of Lincolnshire, but their money-dealing occupation brought with it a certain amount of unpopularity and insinuations including that of charging exorbitant interest rates. There seems little awareness of the fact that the Jews, by royal command, were made to ask for a high percentage on any loan, and that they were also forced to take deeds and goods as a surety for any loan. (11) Such demands tended to alienate the Jews from their fellow citizens. Further problems arose when a Council of the Church, in 1179, passed a decree forbidding any Christian to live with, or be employed by a Jew.

With the beginning of the Crusades, persecution of the Jews increased. In spite of papal and royal protection, their occupation and the conditions imposed upon them made them increasingly unpopular. When Richard I began to prepare a Third Crusade to the Holy Land, this created such fervour that many attacks upon the Jews took place. It is significant that even at Richards coronation, in 1189, an anti-Jewish riot broke out. (12) During the following year a fracas broke out at Stamford, when some aspiring Crusaders attacked local Jews. The trouble then spread to Lincoln where, fortunately, the conspiracy was made public before a full - scale attack could be organised. When the mob was stirred up in Lincoln the Jews found an ally in Bishop Hugh, who defended them and gave them refuge in the castle. However despite Bishop Hugh's intervention several houses were looted, including some in the Dernestall, the Strait, and *up Steep Hill, which opens on the High Street to the west of the old Bull Ring...* (13) When Bishop Hugh died in 1200 the Jewish community rightly mourned the loss of their protector. (14)

Throughout the thirteenth century there were periodic outbreaks of anti Jewish feeling which included the slaying of Moses of Lincoln, in 1220, by Walter de Evermeus men, and the killing of Deulecresse and his wife, Sarra. (15) There was also a certain amount of episcopal and clerical intolerance and the crown intervened in such matters at least twice. On one of these occasions the Archbishop of Canterbury concurred when the Bishop of Lincoln decreed that no one *in their diocese should sell victuals to the Jews or have any communication with them. When the king heard of this he sent letters to the sheriff's commanding them to supply these victual; and other necessaries.* (16) With the stringent conditions and high levies imposed on them by the crown, the Jews led a very uncomfortable life.

The most famous incident in Lincoln, which took place in 1255 is fully dealt with in Chapter 7. Amongst many other incidents one took place in 1266, when some disinherited knights raided a synagogue (by tradition on Steep Hill) and burned the records. This was a disaster both for the Jews, and for following generations of historians deprived of so much documentation of a great part of Lincoln's history. The attacks upon the Jews and the destruction of their records were due to many factors. The Jews like the Muslims were not Christians. They were in a sense enemies of the cross. Sometimes it suited the crown to encourage a wave of persecution from which it could benefit. Often, those finding themselves heavily in debt, destroyed records of the debts they could not repay. The main aim was always to avoid repayment of debt.

Finally, to add to their traumas, the Jews were expelled from England in 1290.

DAVID VALES IMPRESSION OF AREA IN 1180

David Vale said that his sketch is 'An impression looking north as it might have appeared about 1180. The Jews House is shown with shops on the ground floor as is now generally accepted. (Linc. Arch. No 5) The small round headed window is conjectural, the present window being nineteenth century and the one previous (as shown on early prints) being a small pointed opening invented well after the Norman period. I have shown a rather imaginative facade to Jews Court as there appears to be no evidence as to what it looked like in Norman times.

The Cathedral is depicted as it might have looked before the earthquake [1185]. On the right of the picture is St. Cuthbert's Church. There is no evidence as to its appearance, but it was situated opposite the Jews House and [Jews] Court. It would probably have been a fairly small building. The rest of the buildings shown are purely imaginative.'

(Fig 4) Drawing by David Vale of the area as it might have appeared in 1180

CHAPTER THREE
The Norman House

At the corner of Steep Hill and Christ's Hospital Terrace is a medieval building, Norman House, dating from about 1170-1180. Although some historians suggest that it was occupied by Aaron of Lincoln, there is no evidence that he ever lived there. What is known, and recorded in the book of Fees, was that Aaron had land and property within the old gate of the Bail on the west side. (1) Norman House was owned by Joceus or Josce of York up to about 1190. (2) Some property deeds record that, C. 1240, the property was under the ownership of Peter of Legborne, who also had land at Raithby, Tathwell, Saltfleetby, Somercotes and Trusthorpe and appears to have come from the Louth district. The Norman House was then granted, by Peter, to Thorald a cooper whose son, in about 1270, granted it to a doctor, William de Roveston who gave it to the Dean and

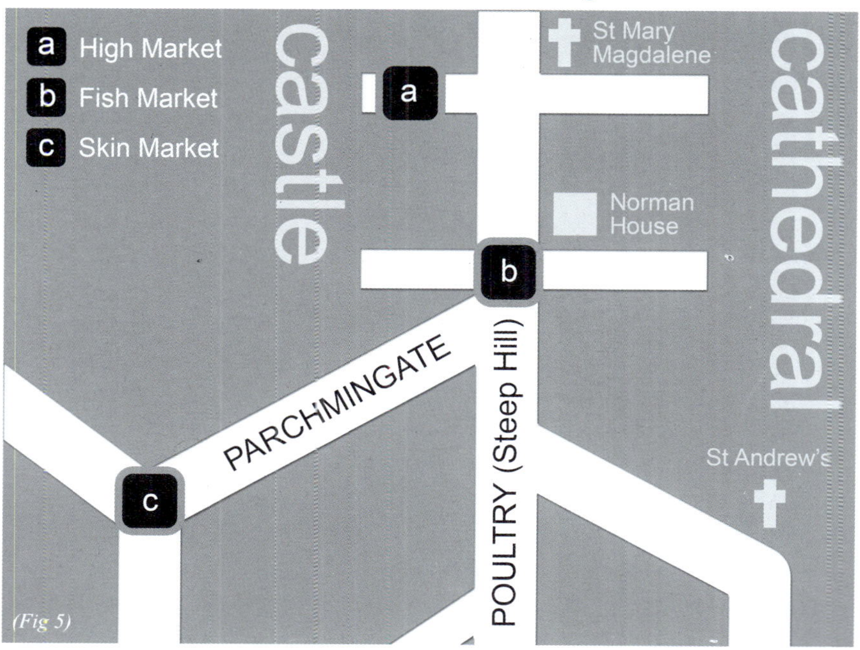

(Fig 5)

(Fig 6) Norman House, showing window which replaced chimney (a) and restored window (b)

Chapter, as part of the endowment of his chantry. (3) Aaron of Lincoln, the great Anglo-Jewish financier, did live in the uphill area, but almost certainly not at the Norman House. Although it is still called by many, even today, Aarons House, this is quite unfounded.

In 1850 it was a butchers shop, but by 1878 the Norman House had obviously become very run down. (4) In March of that year an article appeared in the local press describing how *during the process of restoring an antiquated and dilapidated building on the Steep Hill, an ancient stone window of Norman architecture had been discovered in the front wall.* (5) At this time the property was occupied by Mr. Robert Lee, Newsagent. The window, which had obviously been built over, was carefully preserved and restored by the Governors of Christ's Hospital. The *centre pillar or column of the window was missing* and the Rev. Venables undertook to restore this at his own cost. (6) From about 1896 until 1936 a cobbler, John Borman, carried on his business at Norman House. Canon J.S Caulton, Rector of Burton-by-Lincoln, said that Mr Borman *had made boots for the bishops and deans of Lincoln from 1860.* (7) Canon Caulton

(Fig 7) Norman House, South Wall showing some of the original stone work with the later addition of brick gable ends

was formerly rector of St. Michaels. As Mr Borman was born on April 1 1847 it is possible, that in his early years, he was apprenticed to another cobbler.

It is evident that many alterations have taken place over the years: originally the entrance arch in the middle of the west front had a fireplace buttress above it. The idea of this combination is credited, by Maurice Barley, to the mason who designed the Lincoln Norman houses. (8) The buttress has been replaced by a window. (see fig 6) Note also the restored Norman window. In 1937 the Norman House was divided into three separate dwellings with part of it becoming an antique shop. During the alterations a splendid barrel vault and aumbrey was found in a *semi-underground cellar*. (9) Many other important discoveries were also made at that time including a *Transitional Norman doorway* [which was] *in a good state of preservation*. The bottom jambs of which, along with the stiff leaf foliage decoration of the capitals, had been cut, in order to erect some modern woodwork. Despite this the ball flower ornament of the inner hollow moulding was well preserved. Another unique feature was an internal doorway, dating from between 1170-1180, with a most unusual circular arch with notched stones: this type of stone, common in flat arches, was rarely found in round ones. (10) The proprietor of the antique shop, in 1939, was Mr. G. W. Shelton. The property was divided into four tenements in 1948. Mr. G. Taylor, a cabinet maker, used the premises from then until 1973. In 1974 a firm of Upholsterers R.E. Giddons Ltd. was located there. (11)

Described as one of the oldest inhabited houses in Europe the Norman House was granted an award by the Lincoln Civic Trust in a design competition in 1961. During the 1980s the St. Barnabas Trust had a hospice shop on the premises, and presently it houses the Neustadt wine shop, whilst the undercroft houses a shop, Hemsleys, selling needlecraft. In Illustration 7 note the partially brick-faced south wall with its fragments of a string- course. Roland Harris described the *semi-subterranean undercroft*, of the Norman House, *as being an extremely important and early example of a trend in England towards a more sophisticated type of town-house.* (12)

CHAPTER FOUR
Jews HOUSE

Towards the bottom and on the west side of Steep Hill is the Jews House. It was built earlier than the Norman House, and was then in the parish of St. Cuthbert, and more recently St. Michael. Dating from late 1150 or 1160, it is mentioned in the charters of Lincoln Cathedral and is contemporary with St. Mary's Guildhall, Wigford. Although the Norman House and the Jews House are some two decades apart Roland Harris sees them as providing two very consistent models for the appearance

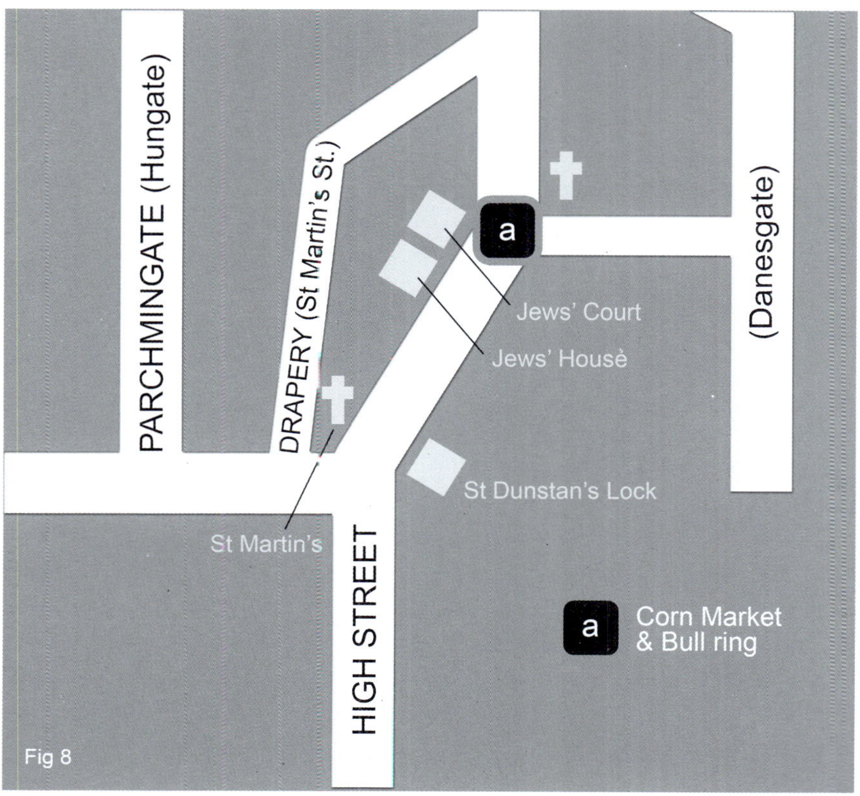

Fig 8

of Romanesque commercial town-houses. (1) The Jews House has been described as being *one of the earliest and most interesting examples of domestic architecture in England*: with the upstairs room (chamber) similar to that at Boothby Pagnell Hall, which is reached by a back staircase. (2) Originally the Jews House was probably similar in design to the medieval merchants house which consisted of a through passage with a room each side and whose chamber was also upstairs.

It is possible that certain features of the Norman House were inspired by the Jews House, in particular the chimney. Supported by a decorative archway over the front door: this is still intact on the Jews House. Originally *the lower part [contained] two flues and fire-places, one on each side of the door, which [united] above the arch into one.* (3) An upstairs fireplace was a notable luxury during medieval times. The original front entrance door would have consisted of one order of shafts, with links of interlaced chain on the arch; and the *richly carved doorway was enhanced by windows which had decorative mouldings.* (4) EJ. Willson, in 1816, thought that some of the mouldings on the doors were reminiscent of the west doors of the Cathedral. (5) Some of the decorative door moulding has now been revealed.

An article, by Willson, in Pugin's *'Specimens'*, referred to a 1724 sketch by Buck, showing the original chimney shaft, which was described as a tall circular tube with a square base having a small triangular gable at each of its sides; the top was shattered and wanted its proper finish. The chimney still forms a very interesting feature in that it is corbelled out over a semi circular arch. A drawing by Twopenny, appeared in Parker's 1851 *'Glossary'*, showing a second two-light window on the upper floor. In 1872 it was thought this window had been destroyed *within the last 20 years.* (6) This gives some idea of the deterioration that had taken place during that period of time.

With the living quarters on the upper storey, space was left at street level for a shop, workshop, or warehouse. It is assumed that the ground floor of Jews House would have, originally, contained shops. An excellent reconstruction, of how the medieval ground floor, complete with its shop fronts, might have looked, has been produced by Roland Harris. (7) The ground floor measurement *north to south, [was] 39ft. 6 in., by 20 ft. east to west*. The front wall was 2 ft. 6 in thick and the back wall was 2ft. 9in. (8) Harris suggested that one can see, despite obscurities, *that the ground floor comprised only three shops c. 4.5 m [14ft] deep, with a central passage*. He also saw that the chimneys off-centre position, and the lack of

(Fig 9) Jews House showing Mazuzah niche

medieval domestic rooms, indicated that *the solar overlooking the street was subdivided, most probably with a greater chamber* at the northern end, functioning as a hall, with *a smaller private chamber to the south.* As the ground floor lacked non-commercial rooms, he further suggested that there would be some ancillary structures, including a *free-standing kitchen in the plot behind the house.* (9)

By the end of the nineteenth century the first floor had three rooms with three attics above and square windows had replaced the ground floor loopholes. But a *curious internal arch* was thought by Arch-Deacon Venables to have been part of the original structure. (10) The front doorway was the main access to the upper chamber, and the capital to the right of the doorway would, originally, have had 2 oval excavations which were 3ft high by 2ft wide with round edges. It is possible this would have housed the Mazuzah: a parchment sacred to the Jews, which was touched, both upon entering and leaving the building, accompanied by the prayer *may God keep my going out and my coming in from now on and for ever more.* (11) *(see fig 9)*

The way in which some of the roof timbers have been re-used gives an indication of how the original roof was formed. Pevsner suggested that *it was of a simple form with collar-beams and the additional support of ashlar pieces near the base of the rafters.* (12) Some work carried out revealed how *three tie-beams from the earlier structure* had been used as ceiling beams to the south of the attic floor. These showed how the medieval tie-beams had been notched at the base for the addition of ashlar pieces in order to strengthen the beams. This find enabled a re-construction to be made of some of the medieval roof details. (13)

(Fig 10) Jews House in the 1930s

Sometime during the late nineteenth and early twentieth century the arch over the doorway had been *filled with modern brickwork*. (14) A report given in 1959 by Mr. Horace Hathaway, a stonemason from Mansfield, showed more evidence of change: *he thought that the whole of the southwest corner [had] been completely rebuilt during the last 150 years*. He reported that the stone used in the restoration came from *an old farmhouse at Burton, near Lincoln*. (15)

The present building contains a restaurant with a small wig shop occupying the room to the right of the central passage. Although the house has undergone many alterations over the years, and it is difficult to determine exactly what the original interior looked like, the building still retains many of its former features particularly on the exterior. Note, for instance, how the window frames of the windows which must have lighted important first-floor windows rise from a long string course and are neatly moulded. (16) (see fig 10)

What of the people who have lived here? One of the earliest residents of Jews House is thought to have been a Jewess called Bellasez, (Chap. 1) the daughter of Rabbi Benedict and grand-daughter of Rabbi Moses. She also had three well known uncles: Hagin, who rose to prominence between 1257 and 1280, becoming the Arch-Presbyter of English Jewry; Jacob who, in 1267, sold Walter de Merton the property which became the site of Merton College Oxford; and Elias who rose to the heights as a prolific writer and physician.(17) A problem exists in that many Jewesses were called Bellasez: therefore did this Bellasez actually live at-Jews House?

When the Jews were expelled in 1290 Bellaset of Wallingford owned the property which was then seized by the King, who later granted it to Walter Ie Foure of Fulletby. The records of the Lincoln Dean and Chapter show how, in 1309, Walter granted two stalls in the corn market of St. Cuthberts parish to Roger le Bower of Newcastle. Roger later sold these to William de Thornton, a canon of Lincoln.

Walter of Fulletby of Lincoln, smith to Roger le Bower of Newcastle, dwelling in Lincoln, of two seldae (shops) in the parish of St. Cuthbert, in the cornemarket...(18)

CHAPTER FIVE
Jews Court

When was Jews Court built?

(Fig 11) Jews House/Jews Court. 19th C sketch from the Willson Collection

Although similar in style to Jews House, with a central passageway, Jews Court has been considerably altered over the years making it difficult to work out what the original building actually looked like. It is known that, during medieval times, Jews House was flanked on the north by land belonging to Henry Brakaldoun and on the south by property owned by Wm de Lonsdale and Adam Aske. (1) Perhaps this helps to substantiate the theory that it was built later than Jews House. How much later, however, is still debatable for the building has had a chequered history and is representative of many periods.

Why is it called Jews Court?

Two suggestions for the origin of the name have been given: its association with the Jews during the medieval period; or that the name became attached to the building at a much later period, when the building was let to several tenants.

Drastic structural change has taken place to Jews Court: for instance, the present internal cross wall was the original outer wall on the west side of the building (see illus. 12), whilst the high window set therein appears to be a sixteenth century feature.

Similar windows are to be found on the east side of the building. The land to the north of Jews Court, until just after the Second World War, contained three shops. Before the present property was built excavations by CLAU were carried out in 1974. However due to the land being on a hill it was difficult to determine any earlier period than late seventeenth to early eighteenth century. (2)

After a survey of Jews Court in the 1990s, CLAU, suggested the possibility of a rebuild between the fifteenth and seventeenth centuries, and their report contained the following hypothesis:

(Fig 12) Jews Court, showing part of the original west outer wall and looking into the present office. View taken from the central passageway

(Fig 13) Jews Court, North Elevation 1974

Original medieval building by 13th century, [possible] 14th century extension, demolished by c.1600. front range rebuilt first; extension added subsequently, by early-mid 17th century. Restoration work 1931-2. (3) Although it is not easy to work out any detailed plan of when alterations actually took place at Jews Court it is known that after its reprieve in 1932 the property underwent a drastic renovation when the whole of the inside *was cleared from cellar to roof, and entirely reconstructed.* (4)

About 1977 the steps leading from the street door were installed and, during the same period, work was carried out at Jews House. This task was undertaken by boys from the Craigland Residential Home for Working Boys under their warden Mr. Marshall. (5)

(Fig 14) Jews Court, 1932 restoration
(By kind permission of the Lincolnshire Echo)

A survey undertaken in 1997, for the Jews Court Trust, revealed that, although there is evidence of some medieval stone, particularly in the cellar, the present building is mainly of the late seventeenth to early eighteenth century. However there are traces and features which date from earlier periods i.e fifteenth and sixteenth centuries including the windows mentioned above.

Robert Pilling, the architect, observed some interesting changes when he compared the present day building with that shown on a post card of c.1900. The post card showed the Jews Court basement north window lintel had *curved ends* that sprung *from its stone reveals*, which are no longer there. He also reported that since the photograph was taken the south of the entrance door had inherited a stone coping and *a tiled offset had been reformed*. It was also noted that the street side first floor window to the north *had a reused Cyma moulde oak lintel* inserted which was possibly fifteenth century. Further to this Mr Pilling noticed how the post card showed the steps from the street rose *to a doorway set in reveal* within which was a Cyma moulded door frame head perhaps of late sixteenth to early seventeenth century. Also revealed were *scars of a third door frame (on the stonework) and timber plugging*; and that *the roof trusses to the main range may have been altered in the late nineteenth century*. (6)

In the late 1990s the removal of some loose plaster, during re-decorating, revealed that the cross wall at the west lend of the passage was possibly late seventeenth to early eighteenth century. It also showed that the doorway itself was the original one supposedly leading to a garden or courtyard. Further work undertaken on the south wall of the present office in 1999 revealed the possibility that a doorway originally occupied the space where a window is now situated. Some of the exterior stonework below ground level was also exposed, and archaeologists from C.L.A.U concluded that there was no actual evidence of any earlier period than late seventeenth to early eighteenth century.

In the year 2000 some masonry samples were taken and subjected to a new method of dating stone buildings. Graham Borradaile using the *viscous remnant magnetization* found that of the samples examined most *were probably reworked late Roman masonry*. He found that *although some samples included pieces of undoubted architectural antiquity this did not include any typical early Norman ages*. The survey also found *evidence of seventeenth to nineteenth century reconstruction or re-modelling, in the period A.D. 1750 to 1850, that involved the removal and re-installation of masonry*. (7)

(Fig 15) Jews Court East Elevation

(Fig 16) Stone exposed on the South Wall of the present office during repair work in 1999. Showing part of the window and sill.

Jews Court at the beginning of the 21st Century

The present passageway leading from the street side, which faces east, is flanked by the S.L.H.A. bookshop on the north side and a second-hand book room, kitchen and toilets on the south side. Jews Court probably had one upstairs room originally and it is possible that a passageway existed to the south of Jews Court leading to Jews House. If this assumption is correct, there could have been an outside staircase where the present indoor staircase is. This would fit in very well with the theory that the doorway of Jews House was the original entrance to the synagogue. However, owing to the fact that the present kitchen and toilet block of Jews Court now occupy the area where, if it existed, this passageway would have joined Jews House, this is difficult to determine.

As the rooms on the west side of the building were evidently built at a later date is it possible that they were added during the seventeenth century when, according to C.L.A.U., some rebuilding took place? (8)

The office situated on the west side of the ground floor is separated by a passageway which runs from the north to the south of the property. The present stairs, to the right of the original back doorway, ascend to the upper chamber, and the present back doorway is situated to the left of this and serves as a fire escape into a courtyard with a garden beyond it. To the left of the upper chamber there are some steps leading to the present library. From the library a doorway gives access to a utility room and stairs leading to the attic.

CHAPTER SIX

The Upper Room (Conference Room)

In 1934, when the Jewish Historical Society visited Lincoln, Dr. Cecil Roth was invited to address a meeting held at Jews Court. An eminent antiquarian, he envisaged the Conference Room of Jews Court as the original Synagogue. (1)

On the eastern wall of the large upper room of Jews Court is a niche, which, as Dr Roth pointed out, is in the correct position where, in a Jewish Synagogue, the Ark (Aron Kodesh) is usually placed. It has been suggested that this gives further credence to Jews Court having housed the Synagogue. The Ark is where the scrolls of the Pentateuch, the first five books of the Bible, are kept.

Whilst the niche may appear to be no more than just a useful cupboard it is, arguably, similar in style to known arks of that period and is certainly ideal for that purpose today. Surviving many episodes of building alteration and repair it measured two and three quarter feet in height by three feet wide, and 1 foot two inches deep. Its base was located two and a half feet above the existing floor level. Helen Rosenau points out that the floor has been raised about 18ins which made it still more suitable as a depository for the Scrolls of the Law. (2)

Dr Roth also drew attention to the point that the only architectural feature necessary in a Jewish Synagogue was an Ark.

Whether or not this niche originally had a religious function it has recently been adapted in order that the Lincoln Jewish Community, who meet regularly at Jews Court, can use it for housing their sacred parchments. Figure 17 shows the architectural design later modified for the new Aron Kodesh.

Dr Roth in emphasizing the place of worship on an upper floor, indicated that the lower rooms of the building would have been occupied by the synagogue officials. Dr Roth also put forward a theory that the doorway of the Jews House was the main entrance to a rear door into the synagogue, as it was much too elaborate for the doorway of a private

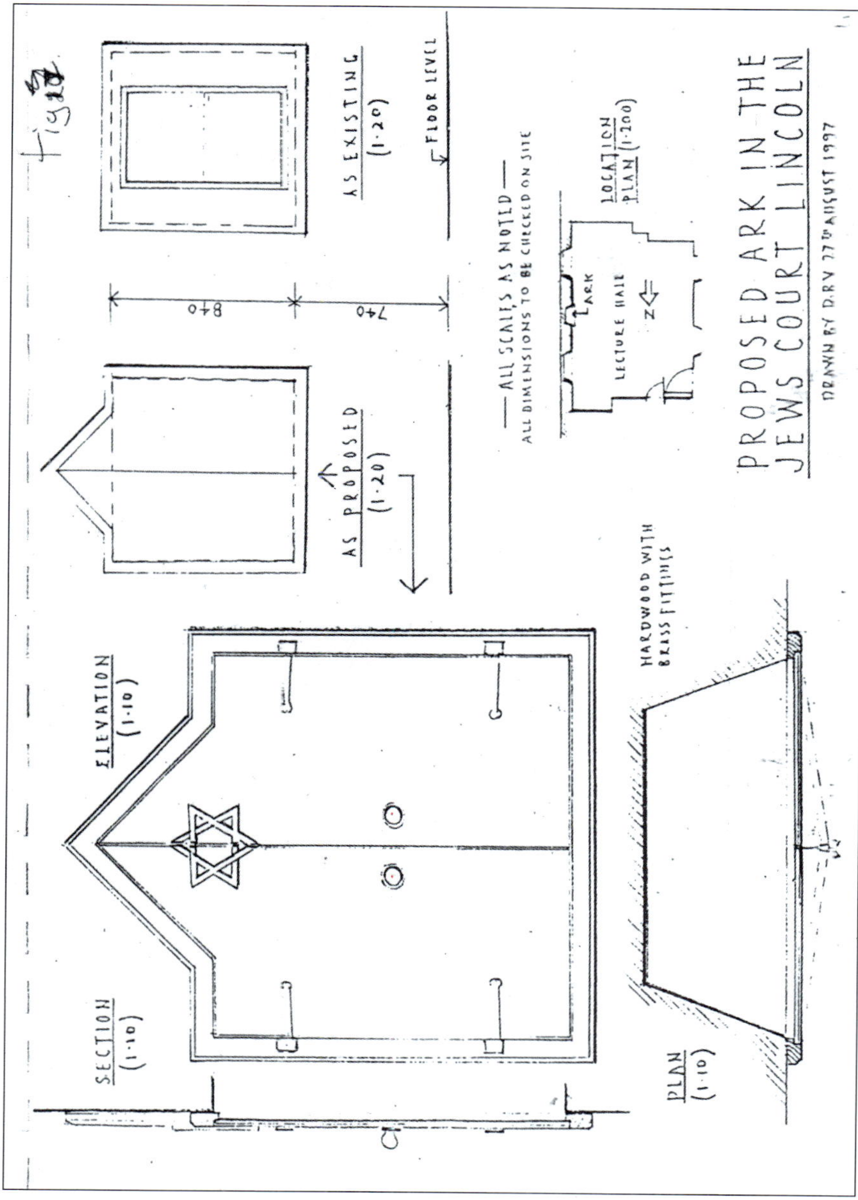

(Fig 17) Architectural Design for Aron Kodesh. (By kind permission of the Jews Court Trust)

house. He saw the property has having the marks of a public building as opposed to that of a private dwelling and the large upper room as being an untold luxury to a middle class household. He also pointed out that the building itself was out of line with the adjacent houses, thus allowing the eastern wall to face more directly towards Jerusalem. (3) The fact that the building is on the line of a natural water course may help to substantiate the argument. Water is a very important part of Jewish worship. A mikvah (ritual bath) used by the Jews was either built directly into the ground, or was an integral part of a building attached to the ground. Although the receptacle for the water could be man made, the water itself was required to be clear, natural water: i.e. a spring, a river derived from springs, a well, the sea, rainwater, snow or melted ice. (4) Jews Court is in an ideal situation for receiving the rainwater coming down Steep Hill which still collects in the cellar of the building.

(Fig 18) The cupboard in Jews Court before 1997/8

CHAPTER SEVEN
The Legend Of Little Saint Hugh

Two aspects of the history of the Jews of Lincoln are associated with Jews Court, one is the synagogue and the other is little Saint Hugh. The latter seems to be foremost in the minds of many tourists who visit the building. The legend that a small boy, Hugh, was found in a well, is part of the original story of 1255. Although other locations have been suggested, tradition indicates a cellar at Jews Court. The first thing many visitors want to know is where the well is or was. Although Lincoln Jews had been subject to many vicious attacks, no action was more bitter than the accusation that, in 1255, they crucified a young Christian boy and threw his body down a well. There is no doubt that a young boy's body was found, although there is no evidence of exactly where. Nor is there any proof as to who perpetrated the ghastly deed. How he met his death remains a mystery. The fact that similar malicious stories were told in such towns as Norwich (1144), Bury-St-Edmunds (1181), Gloucester

(Fig 19) The Shrine of Little St Hugh in Lincoln Cathedral before desecration

(Fig 20) Jews Court East elevation showing rendered walls late 19th Century to early 20th Century

(1168) and York (early 13th C) help to substantiate the belief that the Jews were being persecuted on a national scale. It is assumed that those who accused the Jews of such a crime had ulterior motives. They certainly allowed their prejudice and lack of understanding of Jewish culture to cloud their minds. Any contact with blood, in any shape or form was anathema to the medieval Jew: their stringent kosher laws instructed them to drain and wash all blood from any meat; and another Jewish law forbade Crucifixion: this was a Roman punishment, never Jewish. As a result of the accusation of the murder of little Hugh many innocent Jews were arrested including Benedict, the father of Bellasez (Chap One). He was one of the accused taken to London and imprisoned in the Tower: but was later pardoned. Many others, not so fortunate, were hung, and on Aug 20th 1256 *Simon Passelews and the Sheriff of Lincoln, Wm. de Lergton, were appointed: to sell, by view of testimony of lawful men, the houses [of the Lincoln Jews] who were hanged for the boy crucified there.* (1) Amongst the stories and ballads, which have been told and sung about Hugh, (who was never canonized but, by popular acclaim was called little St. Hugh), was Chaucer's Prioress Tale. Many of these have been translated into other languages and one French ballad contained

87 stanzas, and gave Hughs birthplace as the Demestal: En Nichole.Ja riche citie, Droit en Demestal, l'enfant fut nee. (2) Lincoln, on Norman tongues became Nichole , and Demestal was St. Dunstan's Lock, which was situated at the junction of High Street and the Strait. Another one tells the story of Hugh with a ball, which goes through the window of a Jews House. The following lines are from this ballad:

When bells were rung, and mass was sung,
And all the boys came home,
Then every mother had her son,
But Lady Helen had none.
And all the bells of merry Lincoln
Without mens hands were rung,
And all the books of merry Lincoln,
Were read without mens tongue;
And never was such a burial,
Since Adams days begun. (3)

The *Lincoln Review* quoted a version of the ballad, that Precentor Venables heard as a child in Buckinghamshire, which contained: *But Lady Maisy had none.*

Despite the fact that the story is shrouded in mystery and the politics of the day it has drawn many people to Jews Court. In August 1852., when the British Archaeological Society came to Lincoln to visit Jews House, some members were more interested in Jews Court and the story of Little St. Hugh. (4) The author of an article in a Jewish magazine shows how sceptical he was of the well, said to-have been in the front underground room of Jews Court, and in the upper house [3 Steep Hill] near the fireplace by ending his piece, with a flourish of cynicism: *Add to this that a room on the first floor of the same house is, said to have been used as a synagogue, this is, I think, a fair amount of legendary tradition for one building.* (5) Further influence of this tradition can be seen when, in 1928, Lincoln City Council recommended that Jews Court should be demolished but suggested that the well should be preserved and made available to the public. (6)

Many eminent Lincoln people, over the years, have added their voices in protest over the ongoing 'allegations. Amongst them was Counsellor G Deer, Mayor in 1934, who said that the accusation of 1255 *could be no other than a libel based on the prejudice and ignorance of an unenlightened age.* The Lincoln Diocesan Magazine quoted an extract from an editorial in the Jewish Chronicle of how a visit of the Jewish Historical Society to Lincoln: *a tragic area in Anglo-Jewish History was a delightful experience to those who, participated in it, and a testimony to the admirable spirit of the local Architectural and Archaeological Society, as well as the Mayor [Cllr. Deer], to whose invitation the visit was due.* The editor [of the Jewish Chronicle] expressed the hope that it would be *the forerunner of other and similar pilgrimages*, adding that such visits *renew the links with our ancient story, and fortify afresh our Jewish consciousness.* (7)

In 1959 Dean Dunlop of Lincoln spoke out against *Trumped up stories of ritual murders of Christian boys by Jewish communities [which] were common throughout Europe during the Middle Ages and even much later. The fictions cost many innocent Jews their lives. Lincoln had its own legend, and the alleged victim was buried in the Cathedral in the year 1255. Such stories do not redound to the credit of Christendom and so we pray: Lord forgive what we have been amend what we are and direct what we shall do.* (8)

The above notice is to be found near Little St. Hughs Shrine in Lincoln Cathedral.

Perhaps the following will help to clear up some of the mystery surrounding the well? An article in a local newspaper described how Harry Staples, of Hereward Street, Lincoln, was employed to dig a well, during 1910/1911, for Mr Dodgson the owner of Jews Court. (9) A son, of Mr Whitworth Wright who had a shop at Jews Court during the nineteenth century, confirmed that Mr Dodgson had a well built and said that *it was filled in with water and remained filled by the water draining in from the hill in rainy weather.* (10) In June 1928 an article appeared in the *Lincolnshire Echo* with the heading *The Legend of the Well*. In 1971 another article, regarding the well, appeared in the *Lincolnshire Echo*: Jack Ruddock, a local historian and businessman, found some papers in his family's print works amongst which was an entry ticket reading:

Jews COURT, LINCOLN
ADMIT BEARER TO SEE
ST. HUGHS WELL
ADMISSION THREEPENCE
THIS TICKET TO BE GIVEN TO THE CARETAKER. (11)

With it was a further order, dated 24th September 1913, from Rayner. (12)

In 1981 the *Lincoln Youth Theatre*, performed the story of *Little St Hugh* accompanied by a group called *Yesterday*. Recently the legend has inspired Steven Berkoff, the playwright, to write *Ritual in Blood* which was produced at the Nottingham Playhouse during May and June 2001. This version tells the story of a boy killed when falling from an apple tree in a Jewish money-lender's garden. The boy's body was hidden in a well by his brother, in whose care the boy had been. The brother was believed when he blamed the Jews.

Despite all the interest in the well at Jews Court it is unlikely that such a well existed during medieval times, and it certainly bears no resemblance to the mikvah (a gathering of water) or ritual bath, which is a very important element of Jewish worship. The *neat stone basin* mentioned by Sir Francis Hill appears more in keeping with the mikvah. (13)

With conspiracies instigated by the King and the Church, as well as the people, conditions became increasingly difficult for the Jews and in 1290 they were expelled from England.

CHAPTER EIGHT
The Expulsion

When the Jews were driven out of Lincoln the number of Jewish families was greater than the houses they inhabited. Sixty -six Jewish households were recorded but only 30 houses were seized. (1) By 1275 the Jews had been excluded from most ways of earning a living. Many were forced out of their homes and made to live with other families. So conditions would have been desperate, with poverty and over-crowding commonplace. As several families were living together during this period could this have given the impression of a kind of ghetto in Lincoln? About the same time they were prohibited from lending any more money. This along with not being allowed to trade meant that their means of livelihood was cut off. The community, impoverished by persecution and the anti-usery legislation became the victims of their Royal protector.

At the expulsion from the city their property and effects amounted to about £2,500, a lot of money for that period, all of which came into the possession of the king. Thus after over two centuries of adding to the prosperity of the towns and cities they inhabited, the Jews were herded from England.

Although some Jews converted to Christianity the majority preferred death to giving up their faith and vast numbers were forced to march to the ports where they embarked for France, the Low Countries and Ireland. Whereas some Jews were allowed to take as many possessions as they could carry many more fled empty-handed. Owing to fatigue and lack of food many, particularly the elderly and sick, died en route; and, to add to their hardships, they were often attacked and robbed as they passed through hostile villages.

At the time of the expulsion the Jews House was owned by Belaset, daughter of Solomon of Wallingford, who was hanged. There has been much confusion regarding Bellasez and Belaset, at one time they were thought, by many historians, to be the same person. The author has tried, without success, to track down how many Jewesses of this name were resident in Lincoln during this period and where they lived. However the father of Bellasez, as can be seen in chapter one, was Benedict.

The Jews did not return to England until 1656 when under Oliver Cromwell's protection they were able to provide him with trade links. However long before the end of the nineteenth century Britain had a Jewish Prime Minister in Benjamin Disraeli.

CHAPTER NINE

Residents of a Later Age

Jews House

Before the nineteenth century documentary evidence is sparse. However a lease for No.1 Steep Hill and No. 15 The Strait, which make up Jews House, has been traced. Dated 1st of May 1780, it was for twenty one years and made out to an Isaac Wood. This revealed how one tenement was *in the occupation of Clark cordwainer and Thomas Sweeting or his under tenants ... and that this property was abutting on a tenement belonging to the said Isaac Wood, which was occupied by William West and others.* (1)

(Fig 21) External view of Jews Court South Wall during repair work in 1998

From the trade and street directories, and census returns, that became available from the nineteenth century onwards, it can be seen that both the Jews House and Jews Court have been home to many families and their trades and crafts. Let us look at the Cottam family. Mr Charles Cottam rented the property, in 1929, from the Ecclesiastical Commissioners. The author learned from one of his daughters, Mrs Mould, that her father, a furniture and antique dealer specialising in French polishing, came from a Harby farming family. After learning his trade at Nottingham he returned to Lincoln and set up his business in the building which is presently the Lincoln Tourist Information Centre on Castle Hill. It was there that Mrs Mould was born. With the expiration of his ten year lease Mr. Cottam moved to Jews House where, besides his other trades, he also had an undertaking business. His second son, John, worked with him and, after his father's death in his early fifties, took over the business. When Mrs. Cottam died, also in her fifties, Mrs Mould and another sister went to live at Hykeham. Mrs Mould is the proud possessor of a piece of furniture which was her brother John's first piece of French polishing. Listening to her reminiscing about her time at Jews House it is very obvious that she relished every moment there. She told of how her mother was kept constantly occupied in the very large kitchen; and how the other downstairs room was used as a shop with the workshop being located at number 1 Steep Hill, whose access was gained via a passage between the two. (see Fig. 10)

Mrs Mould described Steep Hill and The Strait as being very self sufficient with a wide variety of shops which fulfilled most of the requirements of the neighbourhood, and remembered that there was an inn, the City Arms, on The Strait. She commented on how run-down Jews Court was at the time she was living on Steep Hill During 1929 an Echo reporter described how very different was the condition of Jews House compared to the *dilapidated state* of its neighbour, Jews Court, *whose windows had gone and for a building of such value it looks neglected beyond words*. (2)

Number 14 The Strait was a newsagents, G.F.M. Stamper, in 1928, only to become a milliners and ladies outfitters by 1932. To the north of Jews Court 1928 found Mrs A. East trading as a baker and confectioner at number 4 Steep Hill, whilst Enoch Cooling ran a grocers shop at number 5. Ruddocks Directory shows that by 1932 the City Arms had extended and occupied 23 & 24 The Strait.

In 1950 Jews House was offered to the City Council and it was estimated that, besides restoration of some of the stonework, roof repairs would cost £100. Although it was thought that *the property would doubtless be somewhat of a liability, nevertheless its preservation as an ancient building was to be desired....* (3) By 1972 numbers 4 to 7 Steep Hill had been demolished and the Jews House presently houses a Restaurant, Number 15 The Strait, whilst a wig maker occupies number 1 Steep Hill.

JEWS COURT

What a pity that a building such as Jews Court should have deteriorated so much for it is very obvious that people who had grown up there had some very fond memories. One of them, Edward Wright, remembers The old house as being very interesting and beautiful and often we have had four or five artists in our yard at one time painting the scene. (4) He also said that, at one time 450 visitors had entered the property coming on a particular day. (5)

Up to the 1850s documentary evidence of Jews Court is very sparse: scraps of information may be deduced from leases of nearby properties and evidence gathered from what was happening generally in Lincoln but there is not much to help the researcher. However by 1851 documentary evidence is much more readily available and with the aid of census returns, street directories, and newspaper articles it is possible to trace many of the inhabitants of Jews Court. These sources have been used to give the following picture:

By the mid nineteenth century the property consisted of several tenements: 2 and 3 Steep Hill and 1 to 5 Jews Court. Numbers 2 and 3 Steep Hill are the present cellars, each with its own doorway, although the one to number 3 is never used now due to there being a long drop from the modern street level. It is more difficult to work out the actual position of the numbers of Jews Court. By 1851 William Wright, bricklayer, was the tenant of the property and lived on the premises with his wife, son and daughter. Other families living there were: Mary Hattersley, a nurse, her daughter and son; Edward Bailey, retired blacksmith, his wife, daughter and three grandsons; Frances Beech, dressmaker, a widow, and her son; Edward Caunt shoemaker, and his nephew. Ann Webster a widow, who was a washerwoman, resided at 3 Steep Hill, and William Hammersley, a chair-maker, and his wife Mary at 2 Steep Hill. (6)

In 1854 Mrs Hammersley had as one of her lodgers George Fieldsend who was quite a character being *a poacher of great notoriety and on the last of his escapades was very badly injured. A surgeon, Mr Thomas Sympson, who attended the injured man described to the Magistrates Court how Fieldsend had lacerated wounds on the left leg and a contused wound on the left side of the forehead, about three inches in length.* He said that the injuries were so bad that three or four days later he had a *severe attack of erysipelas followed by abscesses*. Stephen Hardcastle, the Lincoln Police Superintendent, took the man into custody on Friday 10th February 1854 after he had consulted with the surgeon, but by the following day Fieldsend was dead. The case caused such an uproar amongst the townspeople that an enquiry was held at the Magistrates Court and, although it seemed that the man had died from a heart disease, *a large mob gathered in the vicinity of the gaol and great excitement appeared to prevail through the whole city*. They thought he had died at the hands of the Police Superintendent. However a Testimonial drawn up by Mr T J N Brogden of Silver Street showed Hardcastle had the confidence of the city at large. (7)

The Wright family were still resident at Jews Court in 1857 with William's son, Thomas, a painter and glazier, as the tenant at number 1 Jews Court. In 1877 the tenant is listed as Thomas Whitworth Wright, (it is not clear whether this refers to the Thomas of 1857), who also occupied number 3 Steep Hill, possibly as his shop. He and his wife, Elizabeth, had five sons, one being the Edward mentioned earlier, and one daughter, also called Elizabeth. Another son, Ernest, was born there in the 1870s and later worked at Rustons where his shift began at 6.00 am. (8)

By 1881 number 3 Jews Court was being used as a Mission Room and in 1887 a local directory mentioned St Michael's Mission room as being at Jews Court but no number is given. By 1890 the owner of the building was Christs Hospital (which was situated further up Steep Hill).

By 1891 Thomas Wright's widow had taken over the tenancy and was *living on [her] own means* with four of her sons and her four year old daughter, Edith, with John Martin, a foundry labourer, living at number 4 Jews Court, and William Baldwin, an army pensioner, at number 2 Steep Hill. At the same time numbers 3 and 4 Steep Hill were combined to form one shop for *Kirk Joseph News Agent & Basket Maker.* (9)

An article written about 1894, described Jews Court as being *very closely built up*, so much so that the writer found that it was impossible to properly examine the back of the property on the west side because it was *inhabited by very poor people who have a rooted objection to the invasion of inquisitive and prying strangers*. Being bitterly disappointed, he wrote that contrary to his hopes, the houses although of great antiquity, they were not in any way connected with the period at which the Jews lived in Lincoln. One assumes that the writer realised that Jews Court had been rebuilt and lacked any architectural evidence of a medieval building. It is understood that the building at that time consisted of: *two houses immediately north of Jews House which were divided by some steps leading into a court at the back.* (10)

Another newsworthy incident took place in 1898: Eliza Robinson of

Jews Court was arrested for being drunk and disorderly. The unfortunate woman had also attempted suicide. An entry in one directory of that period shows a tenant by the name of W Robinson was living at number 3 Jews Court. (11)

Mrs Rose Roberts, nee Wright, was born at number 1 Jews Court in 1905 which then had three rooms on the first floor with the rest of the tenements consisting of single-room bed-sitters. Rose, married the manager of Halfords, Jack Roberts, and was the niece of Edward Wright. Some members of the Wright family appeared to have lived there until the property was condemned.

In 1911 the property was conveyed to Edward Hawkswell Dodgson: the papers signed on the 3rd January record the conveyance between Dodgson and the National Provincial Bank for a freehold *messuage or dwelling house known as Jews Court*. Although there were several other part owners at the time it appears that they eventually sold their shares to Dodgson. Upon finishing work as a solicitor at Leeds and retiring to Leamington Spa he had purchased Jews Court for its antiquarian interest. However in 1923 a court order was made for the demolition of the property and it was sold, on behalf of Dodgson's widow, on the 24th April 1925, to the Mayor and Corporation of Lincoln for £300. The property at that time consisted of *1 to 5 Jews Court* and *2 to 3 Steep Hill* ... with number 2 Steep Hill containing *a dwelling house and joint yard* and number 3 *a shop and joint yard*. (12) On Tuesday June 5th 1928 the Lincoln City Council voted that the building should be demolished but as recorded in Chapter 5 *the well was to be preserved and made available to the public*. This report also stated that *the interior has in course of time been very much altered and at the time of its acquisition by the Corporation under the slum clearance scheme in April 1925, was used as tenements*. (13)

Fortunately the Lincoln Architectural and Archaeological Society (L.A.A.S.) took an interest and objected to the demolition of such an historic building. As a result the Council decided to give the building to the Society *on condition that they restore and maintain the building to the satisfaction of the Council* and that it should no longer be used as a residential property. The business took longer to transact than was expected and the L.A.A.S. was still awaiting the hand - over of the property in May 1931. However by December of that year a fund-raising committee was formed and repairs were then carried out. Although the exterior walls were worthy of preservation the interior required complete removal: Thompsons of Derby were engaged as architects and Wrights of Lincoln as the builders. A great deal of work was undertaken before the building housed its first tenants. The Lincoln Diocesan Offices shared the tenancy with the Lincolnshire Probation Services Area Committee. When the latter relinquished their lease of the offices, in 1961, the Diocesan Committee took the lease of all the building. Over the years many repairs and improvements have been implemented including major repairs to the boiler, in 1962, at a cost of £56.3s.1d; and by October 1964 the north wall, *particularly at the NE. corner had received attention.* (14)

The Jews Court Trust Minute Book (lC.T. M.B.) showed how the building had created a great deal of interest in that many visitors to Lincoln requested to look around the property. A letter from the Secretary of the Diocesan Board for Social Work. in 1963, emphasised this point and suggested that a plaque might be produced giving information about Jews Court. In reply to this request a pamphlet was prepared shortly afterwards, by Joan Varley, giving information about both Jews House and Jews Court.

In 1965 the L.A.A.S. received an application from the Diocesan Board for Social Work, for improved toilet and washing facilities. A proposal, drawn up by the builders, Messrs. C. R. Lucas & Son was accepted and a request made for a contribution from the Diocesan Board of Finance.

When the L.A.A.S. amalgamated with the Lincolnshire Local History Society (L.L.H.S.) in 1966 the meeting, chaired by F. T. Baker, reported that a new constitution for the new L.L.H.S had been drawn up. In 1974 following further mergers the L.L.H.S. became known as the Society for Lincolnshire History and Archaeology (SLHA). At the same time the Jews Court Trust was set up to take care of the building and its assets and they still are the owners of Jews Court. (15)

From the Trust minute book details of the maintenance work undertaken can be gleaned. In 1968 the repairing of windows and their sills, and external painting was undertaken by Messrs Simons. Also a new heating system, installed by the tenants, had necessitated the dismantling and re-building of the chimney - stack which was in a bad condition. The problems did not end there for in 1971 the trustees were faced with repairs to the exterior of Jews Court and a grant of up to £850 was made by the Historic Buildings Council to cover half the cost of the repairs. From 1974 the building was leased to Lincolnshire and South Humberside Arts. A change of use, to a craft centre, made it necessary for further internal alterations to be carried out. As Jews Court is a grade I listed building, consent was necessary for these repairs and planning permission required for a change to retail use. This renovation included repairs to the sliding sash windows and sills, and the restoration of the store walls and roof. By August 1978 the Jews Court Trust had become a registered charity.

The exterior of Jews Court was re-painted in 1980, and in 1984, owing to a change in their policies, the Lincolnshire and Humberside Arts found it necessary to terminate their lease. Several businesses were interested in the premises at this time amongst them were Mrs Gwen White of Whites Restaurant, Jews House, for use as a restaurant and exhibition area; and John Barralle of Welton for a glass blowing workshop and exhibition area and Christopher Goddard of Bail gate for a studio. However, the next tenant was the St Barnabas Trust, who took over the lease in 1985. When they did not renew their lease the next tenants were, and remain, the Society of Lincolnshire History and Archaeology. The lease being taken on by its trading arm: Lincolnshire Heritage Ltd from 2nd Dec. 1987.

Mr Robert Johns, who had previously used one of the basement rooms for teaching the guitar, requested to be allowed to use it again after the Society took over the lease but, due to rules regarding sub-letting, was refused. Further work was deemed necessary in 1988/89 when a de-humidifier had to be installed in the cellar, and a two-stage renovation began. A report in June 1994 shows that repairs to the north wall and surrounding trees, and shop window repairs had been accomplished. By February 1996 further work had been completed by Richard Lucas, of CR. Lucas & Sons, builders. (16) In 1999 more work was undertaken in the garden when, a group of SLHA volunteers, led by Chairman, Neville Birch, removed an overgrown tree etc which had become hazardous.

(Fig 22) The 1977 steps were painted by Fred Felstead in 1980s or 1990s (member)

(Fig 23) Present day west elevation

(Fig 24) Chairman Neville Birch and volunteer Paul Hunter during removal of overgrown tree in 1999

The building housed a great number of people during the mid-19th century and there was a large turnover of tenants during that period: with some coming from overseas as well as from many parts of Great Britain. Thomas Whitworth Wrights birthplace was Boston, John Martin, was born in Horncastle, and some residents were born in various parts of Lincolnshire including Kirton, Market Rasen, Louth, Sleaford, Wellingore, Brant Broughton and Sutterton. Others came from further afield: Mrs Charlotte Martin, wife of John, came from Curragh Camp, Ireland; and Mrs Jane Sheldon, married to John Sheldon, a retired locomotive engine driver resident at number 2 Jews Court at one time, was born in Heligoland (she later became a British citizen). (17)

It appears that things have come full circle for although people from other countries no longer actually live in the building it is home to so many members, of the S.L.H.A., both in the British Isles and overseas. The Society is proud to have such a prestigious building for their headquarters.

CHAPTER TEN
From the Medieval Synagogue to the Manchester Jewish Museum

Is Jews Court on the original site of a synagogue?

There is some evidence that there was a synagogue on Steep Hill which points to the possibility that Jews Court is built on its site. A charter of 1291 mentions the granting of a 'schola', in St Cuthbert's parish, to Robert de Leverton, along with some other property which had formerly belonged to Benedict, the son of Arabella. Some land in the corn market was also referred to, in deeds of 1316 and 1344, as being *where the Jews school used to be.* (1) This indicates that the school was demolished between 1291 and 1316. The plot indicated is described as being north of the Jews House, but on the south and to the west of the lane known as the Drapery (now known as St Martin's Street).

(Fig 25) A view of the garden of Jews Court before th tree was removed

As a synagogue was often used for educational, as well as' religious. purposes, it was sometimes called a schola (school). The teachers were usually Rabbis, and students or *scholars*, who sometimes included Christians, studied Hebrew and Arabic along with arithmetic and medical science. (2) Archaeological investigations carried out to the north of Jews Court in 1974/5 uncovered signs of an earlier medieval structure However, they were *of less substance than might be expected of a schola* (3) It is therefore possible that the foundations of Jews Court are also the foundations of the original 12th century building that housed the synagogue. If so it is likely that it is the Synagogue of Peyterin (Peitevin) the Great (Chief Rabbi) which features in the story of *Little St Hugh*, and traditionally thought to have been on Steep Hill. An account appears in the Patent Rolls of enquiries which were being made about Jews who belonged to it. (4) It is probable that this was the synagogue attacked by some disinherited knights in 1266. (Chap 2) Peitevin was reputed to have been a financier who did business with Bardney Abbey.

Although the upper walls of the building were obviously altered, renovated or even rebuilt in later centuries, there is no reason to suggest that they followed a different ground plan. Recent studies, undertaken by archaeologists and architects, tend to date the present restructuring of Jews Court as being late 17th to early 18th century. There are however traces of older stone in the cellar, and on the external south wall of Jews Court where structural repairs, undertaken in 1998, exposed re-used fragments of a medieval date, but it was impossible to detect whether they came from an original building or not. Without an in-depth survey, it is not possible to be certain whether it is part of an original building on the site, or brought from elsewhere like the stone used in the restoration of Jews House. (Chap 4)

(Fig 26) Possibly medieval stone but it could have been from another building

Some Jewish historians, including a leader of the present local Lincoln Jewish Community suggest that the synagogue, known to have been on Steep Hill, may have stood in or near the present rear garden of Jews Court. The garden was, and is, very important to Jewish worship, with betrothals and weddings often being celebrated there. Medieval Jews often tended to build their synagogues away from the main thoroughfare: for example at Norwich. However as the residents of Jews House were becoming well known and prosperous, and had permanent stone built places of business that included shops, they were unlikely to be afraid of having their place of worship where it could be seen.

(Fig 27) Inside Manchester Synagogue Museum (By kind permission of its Curator)

Some property deeds belonging to the Gare and Thornton chantry indicated that there was another synagogue at Hungate. This was in St Martin's parish and was located at the top of the High Street. It was built by Elias Martin and was seized by the Crown after the Little St Hugh incident in 1255. (Chap 7) (5)

What would Lincoln's medieval synagogue have looked like? Although there is very little archaeological evidence for medieval synagogues in England, a synagogue in Prague built in the last quarter of the 13th Century, gives some idea: the lowest part is a lower lengthwise vewstibule with broken barrel vaulting. (6)

Raphael Isserlin, a Jewish archaeologist, has pointed out that one of the reasons for the lack of early Jewish synagogues in England is that they were often rebuilt or converted as churches. (7) A good example of what a synagogue would have looked like is to be found at the Jewish Museum in Manchester.

CONCLUSION

This has been an attempt to trace some of the history of the Jews of Lincoln and three of the buildings associated with them. Lack of documentary evidence has meant that large gaps in our knowledge are unfilled and many questions, alas, left unanswered. Little is readily accessible of the history of the houses between the expulsion of the Jews in 1290 and the 19th century making it necessary to offer theories and suppositions. The research has been enlightening and makes one realise that theories of past historians, though discounted by later scholars, retain interest and have some value. These theories help to add colour to the story of these interesting buildings, the people who lived in them and to an area steeped in history.

It is hoped that the reader will enjoy this booklet and find something of interest therein and so be encouraged to pursue the trail by further reading.

(Fig 28) Jews Court
(Drawn by Gerry Lewis, a member of SLHA)

CHAPTER 1

1. ADLERS TRANSCRIPT
2. JOHN WILFORD, SHIDDUKHIMTENNAIM AT JEWS COURT
3. IBID
4. MARKET RASEN MAIL AUGUST 201993

CHAPTER 2

1. TRANSACTIONS OF THE JEWISH HISTORICAL SOCIETY 1894/8; 185/6 (L.C.L.L.S.S) L. LINC. 296
2. SIR FRANCIS HILL, MEDIEVAL LINCOLN 217
3. IBID, 233/4
4. HILL, 153/6
5. IBID, 234
6. HILL, 233
7. E.I. ABELL, LINCOLNSHIRE CHRONICLE & LEADER SEPTEMBER 61930
8. HILL, 23314
9. IBID, 218/20
10. LINCOLNSHIRE ECHO, 1977
11. ABELL (1), 6/8
12. HILL 188/9
13. JOSEPH CLAYTON ST. HUGH OF LINCOLN
14. HILL 223/4
15. CALENDAR OF PATENT ROLLS 1255
16. C. ROTH MEDIEVAL LINCOLN JEWRY AND ITS SYNAGOGUE 26

CHAPTER 3

1. HILL,220
2. ROLAND HARRIS THE Jews HOUSE AND NORMAN HOUSE, LINCOLN ARCHAEOLOGY 5.
3. E.I. ABELL, JEWS OF MEDIEVAL LINCOLN 113A (JEWS OF MED. LIN.)
4. W & B BROOKE SURVEY OF THE ANTIQUITIES OF THE CITY OF LINCOLN 14
5. E.I. ABELL, JEWS OF MED. LIN. REV. BINNALLS CUTTINGS 21

6. IBID 22
7. LINCOLNSHIRE CHRONICLE 28/12/62
8. MAURICE BARLEY, HOUSES AND HISTORY.
9. LINCOLNSHIRE CHRONICLE 13/3/37
10. IBID
11. STREET DIRECTORIES, LINCOLNSHIRE CENTRAL LIBRARY
12. HARRIS

CHAPTER4

1. HARRIS
2. MORTON ILLUSTRATED GUIDE TO LINCOLN 1907.
3. EXLEY
4. NIKOLAUS PEVSNER & JOHN HARRIS LINCOLNSHIRE 519
5. E.J. WILLSON, A HISTORY OF LINCOLN
6. ABELL, JEWS OF MED. LIN.
7. HARRIS
8. JEWISH HISTORICAL SOCIETY JOURNAL (J.R.S ..J) 1894/1898 185
9. HARRIS
10. J.H.S.J 1894/1898 185 (This can still be seen in the wig shop.)
11. LINCOLNSHIRE ECHO JULY 1940
12. PEVSNER 519
13. STANLEY JONES, SURVEY OF ANCIENT HOUSES 25TH L.C..T. REPORT
14. EXLEY, TRANSCRIPT OF Jews COURT & Jews HOUSE LEASES archi ves
15. LINCOLNSHIRE CHRONICLE, 4 SEPTEMBER 1959 ABELL 57
16. BRYAN LITTLE, ARCHAEOLOGY IN NORMAN, BRITAIN 15112
17. ROTH MED. JEWRY & ITS SYNAGOGUE 53
18. LINCOLNSHIRE ARCHIVES OFFICE.. D&C Dij/74/3/4 1-907 CANT. 281

CHAPTER 5

1. ANNALLES OF LINCOLNSHIRE 2 (LINCOLN CITY LIBRARY)
2. C.L.A.U. REPORT 1974

3. C.L.A.U. SURVEY REPORT 1990S
4. ABELL 82 (LINCOLN CITY LIBRARY) REPORT FROM S.M. LIN. OCTOBER 1932
5. Information given to author, when Secretary to the S.L.H.A" by a visitor
6. ROBERT PILLING, ARCHITECTS REPORT
7. GRAHAM BORRADAILE, VISCOUS REMNENT MAGNETIZATION REPORT
8. AS 3 ABOVE

CHAPTER 6

1. CYRIL ROTH
2. HELEN ROSENAU, NOTES ON THE RELATIONSHIP OF Jews COURT AND THE LINCOLN SYNAGOGUE., ARCHAEOLOGICAL JOURNAL 93, 1936
3. ROTH
4. S. KADISH, EDEN IN ALBION, BUILDING JERUSALEM

CHAPTER 7

1. CALENDAR PATENT ROLLS 1256
2. THOMAS. R. HEWITT. Jews COURT & THE LEGEND OF LITTLE ST. HUGH OF LINCOLN
3. IBID
4. LINCOLNSHIRE CHRONICLE AUGUST 1852
5. JEWISH CHRONICLE
6. LINCOLNSHIRE CHRONICLE JUNE 61928
7. LINCOLN DIOCESAN MAGAZINE MARCH 1962 (JEWISH CHRONICLE JUNE 291934)
8. DAILY TELEGRAPH OCT. 15 1959
9. LINCOLN CHRONICLE 1923
10. IBID
11. LINCOLNSHIRE ECHO SEP. 10 1971
12. IBID
13. SIR FRANCIS HILL, MEDIEVAL LINCOLN 232

CHAPTER 8

1. SHARMAN KADISH BUILDING JERUSALEM

CHAPTER 9

1. LEASE OF Jews COURT D.N.U.116/11 (LINCOLNSHIRE ARCHIVES)
2. LINCOLNSHIRE ECHO SEP. 10 1929
3. IBID 29/9/1950
4. ABELL JEW.:> OF MEDIEVAL LINCOLN 1 (CUTTING FROM LINCS. LEADER)
5. IBID
6. LINCOLN CENSUS RETURNS 1851
7. LINCOLNSHIRE, NORTHAMPTON RUTLAND, & NOTTINGHAM ADVERTISER. MARCH 1854
8. FLORENCE. J. BAKER MEMORIES OF LIFE AT JEWS COURT LINCOLN 1905-1928
9. CENSUS RETURNS 1891
10. JEWISH CHRONICLE 1894
11. LINCOLNSHIRE ECHO 22/08/1998 (Report of 1898) .
12. LEASE OF Jews COURT (D.N.U 116/11)
13. LINCOLNSHIRE ECHO JUNE 1928
14. Jews COURT TRUST MINUTE BOOK
15. IBID
16. J.C.T. MINUTE BOOK
17. LINCOLN CITY DIRECTORIES & CENSUS RETURNS

CHAPTER 10

1. DEAN & CHAPTER OF LINCOLN MS/69 f 168 v NO 544
2. LINCOLNSHIRE ARCHAEOLOGY JOURNAL 1946/47
3. CITY OF LINCOLN ARCHAEOLOGY UNIT (CLAU) ANNUAL REPORT 1974/5
4. CALENDAR PATENT ROLLS 1256/59
5. C PC JOHNSON A SECOND JEWISH SCOLA IN LINCOLN SOCIETY FOR LINCOLNSHIRE HISTORY AND ARCHAEOLOGY VOL 13 1978
6. FROM MATERIAL SUPPLIED BY THE PEGGY LANG CENTRE.
7. RAPHAEL ISSERLIN BUILDING JERUSALEM IN THE ISLANDS OF THE SEA.

FURTHER READING

HILL. F, MEDIEVAL LINCOLN Watkins 1990 (reprint)
PEVSNER. N & HARRIS. J, BUILDINGS OF ENGLAND LINCOLNSHIRE (2ND EDITION), Penguin 1990 (reprint)

ARTICLES

BAKER. FJ., MEMORIES OF LIFE AT Jews COURT (SLHA Newsletter)
DAVIS. M.D, THE MEDIEVAL JEWS OF LINCOLN, Archaeological Journal xxxviii
HARRIS. R, Jews HOUSE & NORMAN HOUSE, Lincoln Archaeology 5 (CLAU),
ISSERLIN. RM.J., BUILDING JERUSALEM IN THE ISLANDS OF THE SEA, Building Jerusalem
JOHNSON.C.P.C., A SECOND JEWISH SCOLA IN LINCOLN, Lincolnshire History & Archaeology 13 (S.L.H.A. 1978)
JONES. M.K., MEDIEVAL HOUSES OF FLAXENGATE LINCOLN. Archaeology Of Lincoln. Volll no. 1
JONES. S, HOUSES IN EASTGATE, PRIORY GATE AND JAMES STREET LINCOLN CIVIC TRUST, 25 1974
KADISH. S, THE ARCHAEOLOGY OF MEDIEVAL ANGLO-JEWRY Building Jerusalem
ROSENHAU.H, NOTES ON THE RELATIONSHIP OF Jews COURT AND THE LINCOLN, SYNAGOGUE. ARCHEOLOGICAL JOURNAL 93 1936
WILFORD. J., SHIDDUKHIMTENNAIM AT Jews COURT, S.L.H.A. Past & Present 7 (S.L.H.A.) 1992
WOOD. M. E, NORMAN DOMESTIC ARCHITECTURE, Arch. Journal 92 1935

NEWSPAPERS

LINCOLNSHIRE CHRONICLE & LEADER SEPTEMBER 6 1930
LINCOLNSHIRE ECHO JUNE 1928

MARKET RASEN MAIL AUGUST 20 1993
(others as in sources)

LINCOLNSHIRE ARCHIVES
EXLEY LEASEIDEEDS OF SALE OF Jews COURT (transcript)
Local Studies Department Central Library L.S.c.L.
ABELL, JEWS OF MEDIEVAL LINCOLN
ANNALES LINCOLNIENSES 1&2
CENSUS RETURNS
CRITCHS ANNUAL 1909-10
LINCOLN CITY STREET DIRECTORIES
MORTON, LINCOLN ROYAL SHOW 1907
ROTH. c., ESSAYS AND PORTRAITS IN ANGLO-JEWISH HISTORY
ROTH. c, MEDIEVAL LINCOLN JEWRY & ITS SYNAGOGUE
Transactions of Jewish Historical Society 1895/1895.
WILLSON E.J., THE HISTORY OF LINCOLN

RAKUSEN'S
MATZOS

(Fig 31) The Ark after renovation